ALLEN SMITH

# Memorizing the Parable of the Prodigal Son

*Memorize Scripture, Memorize the Bible, and Seal God's Word in Your Heart*

First published by Nelaco Press 2021

Copyright © 2021 by Allen Smith

All rights reserved. No part of this publication may be reproduced, stored or transmitted in any form or by any means, electronic, mechanical, photocopying, recording, scanning, or otherwise without written permission from the publisher. It is illegal to copy this book, post it to a website, or distribute it by any other means without permission.

Scripture quotations are from The ESV® Bible (The Holy Bible, English Standard Version®), copyright © 2001 by Crossway, a publishing ministry of Good News Publishers. Used by permission. All rights reserved.

First edition

ISBN: 978-1-952381-47-8

This book was professionally typeset on Reedsy. Find out more at reedsy.com

# Contents

| | |
|---|---|
| Before You Begin | 1 |
| Introduction | 2 |
| How To Use This Book | 5 |
| Week 1 Prep Work | 7 |
| Luke 15:11 | 10 |
| Luke 15:12 | 12 |
| Luke 15:13 | 14 |
| Luke 15:14 | 16 |
| Luke 15:15 | 18 |
| Luke 15:16 | 20 |
| Week 2 Prep Work | 23 |
| Luke 15:17 | 25 |
| Luke 15:18 | 27 |
| Luke 15:19 | 29 |
| Luke 15:20 | 31 |
| Luke 15:21 | 33 |
| Luke 15:22 | 35 |
| Week 3 Prep Work | 37 |
| Luke 15:23 | 39 |
| Luke 15:24 | 41 |
| Luke 15:25 | 43 |
| Luke 15:26 | 45 |
| Luke 15:27 | 47 |
| Luke 15:28 | 49 |
| Week 4 Prep Work | 51 |
| Luke 15:29 | 53 |

| | |
|---|---|
| Luke 15:30 | 55 |
| Luke 15:31 | 57 |
| Luke 15:32 | 59 |
| Conclusion | 61 |

# Before You Begin

Hey reader, before you begin memorizing scripture, I wanted to say thank you by offering a free gift.

I wrote a book called Memorize the Sermon on the Mount and I'd like to give you a free copy.

Simply text BIBLE to (678) 506-7543 and I'll send you a free copy straight to your inbox.

I've even thrown in a free bonus gift just for you.

I pray it becomes a blessing to you as you seal God's Word in your heart.

# Introduction

I would like to start off by saying that I have prayed for you, whoever you are, wherever you are, as you are just beginning to start this journey to memorize a piece of the Bible.

In this book, you're going to memorize the parable of the Prodigal Son.

The parable of the Prodigal Son is a beautiful story representing the forgiveness and restoration God has for his children even when they turn from Him. As the story goes, a man has two sons and one of them asks for his inheritance before his father has even died. This was a huge sign of disrespect in their day and certainly still in ours. Not only does he request his inheritance but he also leaves home. This was unheard of at that time considering the father, as the figurehead of his household, reigned supreme. Such an act would result in a total shunning from his father and from society.

The son, armed with his inheritance, lives in sin as he pleasures whatever his flesh desires before running completely out of funds. Before long, he's living amongst pigs. He eventually comes to his senses and decides to return home to his father's house, turning back to where he belongs and away from a life of sin. He has a full speech ready to go once he comes face to face with his father. He feels unworthy of being called his son and is going to plead to be hired on as a servant.

## INTRODUCTION

Upon his return, his father sees him off in the far distance and begins running after him before embracing his son and kissing him. These are not the actions of a father who has disowned his son nor written him off. These are the actions of a father who has been waiting patiently, longing for the return of his son.

Before the son could even begin his prepared speech, his father is giving orders to his servants to prepare a celebration for the return of his son. This paints a lovely picture of just how eager God is to forgive if we would just turn back to him. How pigs are perfectly happy living in mud and amongst other swine but how a true son of God won't. The son of God may live in sin for a time but will eventually come to realize they are not where they belong. And though we may turn back toward God and away from sin, our approach is filled with guilt and shame realizing just how unworthy we are of our title as sons and daughters of God. Though we may feel like hanging our head down low, God sees this as a time to celebrate. But why? Because we've already been forgiven. We've been made righteous before God thanks to the death of Christ on the cross and through His resurrection from the grave. All we were asked to do was to accept the free gift of salvation resulting in being filled with the Holy Spirit marking the beginning of an eternal adoption.

What an incredible and loving God we have who is rich in mercy and grace making this a passage worth memorizing by heart.

It will take some work on your part to commit the passage to memory.

This is a game of repetition over time and there is no guesswork. This book will guide you every step of the way.

That said, there are no tricks, magic strategies, or brain hacks to make it work.

It just takes work but work that is incredibly rewarding.

But even with all that said, there are probably excuses piling up in your head.

Little lies telling you a thousand reasons why you can't possibly remember a section of the Bible.

"I have a bad memory."

"I don't have enough time."

And many other reasons why you might tell yourself this won't work.

Memorizing a passage of the Bible can feel daunting but you don't need to start off by memorizing everything at once.

You just need to start with one verse.

And with that, you're ready to head to the next chapter to learn how to use this book.

## How To Use This Book

By now you are probably curious how this book will work so I will quickly give you an overview.

This book covers the entire parable of the Prodigal Son in the book of Luke, English Standard Version.

This passage of scripture is broken down verse by verse and I recommend you memorize one verse each day working your way through memorizing the entire passage.

Each verse has one dedicated chapter and as mentioned before, this book uses the ESV (English Standard Version) translation. You will be guided to either repeat or recite a verse or verses during each chapter.

This book is set up so that you don't need to have your Bible in front of you to read from.

There are a handful of chapters, though optional, that are the weekly preparation chapters involving some optional prep work. This prep work will make memorizing the entire passage significantly easier and time well spent on your journey to memorizing God's Word. I highly recommend you do it, but feel free to skip it.

Also, I do not require you to say the verse number when memorizing scripture. The original scriptures were not numbered into verses so I don't believe that is a critical piece to remember. However, if you would like to state the verse number when reciting each verse, you are more than welcome to.

As you work your way through memorizing each verse, there will be days where you will get frustrated. It will seem the verse just won't stick. That is completely normal. Some verses will be significantly harder to memorize than others. That is okay. Don't be afraid to repeat a chapter if you feel you didn't quite memorize the verse that day.

If the first round of repetition didn't help it stick, the second or third round should surely do the trick.

You are ready to begin on a wonderful, spirit-filled journey to solidifying a piece of God's Word inside of your heart.

May it be an incredible blessing on your life and your personal walk with Christ.

# Week 1 Prep Work

Welcome to the preparation work on your journey to memorizing The Story of the Prodigal Son.

Like I mentioned in the introduction, this work is completely optional, but I cannot encourage you enough to do the prep work.

If you had four hours to chop down a tree with a dull axe, you would be better off sharpening your axe for two of those four hours before getting started.

This prep work is sharpening your axe.

It will make everything moving forward significantly easier.

Though it will take time, this will be time well spent which you may not realize until you begin memorizing each verse one by one.

To complete the prep work, you will need to read the passage out loud 50 times.

Sounds daunting, doesn't it?

Reading out loud the parable of the Prodigal Son would take roughly 4 minutes. Do that 50 times and you are looking at roughly 3 hours and 20 minutes worth of reading out loud.

Not many people would have the luxury in spare time to squeeze that in and I'm not asking you to.

Instead of doing the entire passage in one go, you are going to do a smaller chunk that would allow you to accomplish the task in an hour or less.

You are going to focus on just the first six verses as you read them out loud 50 times.

Don't have an hour?

Do it for 30 minutes running through them 25 times.

Or commit to what you can. I assure you, whatever you do here will help.

Whenever you try to memorize something from scratch, it can feel like there is a lot of resistance to get the material to stick in your brain.

But if you are very familiar with whatever you are trying to commit to memory, it is like globbing memory glue on it before you get started.

After each week, you will have an opportunity to attempt the next block of 6 verses for the following week.

If you have decided to do the prep work, get ready to read the following chunk of verses out loud. Oh, and grab a glass of water. Your mouth can get pretty dry doing this prep work.

Please note, I left the verse numbers in the passage on the following page for your reference only.

When you are ready, begin.

11 And he said, "There was a man who had two sons. 12 And the younger of them said to his father, 'Father, give me the share of property that is coming to me.' And he divided his property between them. 13 Not many days later, the younger son gathered all he had and took a journey into a far country, and there he squandered his property in reckless living. 14 And when he had spent everything, a severe famine arose in that country, and he began to be in need. 15 So he went and hired himself out to one of the citizens of that country, who sent him into his fields to feed pigs. 16 And he was longing to be fed with the pods that the pigs ate, and no one gave him anything." (Luke 15:11-16 ESV)

See you tomorrow!

# Luke 15:11

Today we are going to memorize Luke 15:11.

You are going to memorize the verse by using the 10-10-10 method.

To use this method, each verse will be repeated out loud 10 times and then immediately recited 10 times from memory. In later chapters, you'll start combining verses and reciting those 10 times as well.

Don't worry if that was a little confusing to follow. Just follow the instructions and you will do just fine.

I understand 10 times may seem excessive and tedious, but trust me, this is necessary. There will be times where it may take you speaking a verse 5 times or more just to fully nail it down before being able to recite it from memory.

As the last word before you begin, I wanted to share with you a few tips that have helped me memorize scripture:

1. Speaking the verse with conviction or emotion as you repeat or recite it from memory.
2. Emphasizing a different word each time you say it out loud.
3. Use hand motions as you speak.
4. Creating images in your head corresponding to each piece of a verse.

5. Singing a verse or a piece of a verse instead of speaking it.

Yes, you heard that last one right. It's weird, it works, but don't feel you need to incorporate all of these at once or any at all. As you go deeper into memorizing scripture, you will find what works for you and what doesn't.

Let's begin.

Say the following verse out loud ten times. You do not have to say the citation within the parenthesis.

**"And he said, 'There was a man who had two sons'" (Luke 15:11).**

When you are done, recite the verse ten times in a row from memory, doing your best not to look at the verse.

Great job! You got your first verse down!

Throughout your day when you are driving your car, taking a break from work, or cooking a meal, go over what you've memorized so far to keep reinforcing it in your mind.

Tomorrow you'll quickly review what you learned today and add another verse to it.

If you don't feel confident you've truly memorized today's verse, consider going through the chapter again.

See you tomorrow!

God Bless.

# Luke 15:12

Today we are going to memorize Luke 15:12.

After you review what you have already learned, you are going to memorize today's verse using the 10-10-10 Method.

Let's begin.

Let's review the verse you learned yesterday by reciting it 10 times from memory. Glance over it if you need a refresher.

**"And he said, 'There was a man who had two sons'" (Luke 15:11).**

When your review is done, let's get into today's verse.

Say the following verse out loud 10 times.

**"'And the younger of them said to his father, "Father, give me the share of property that is coming to me." And he divided his property between them'" (Luke 15:12).**

When you are done, recite the verse 10 times in a row from memory, doing your best not to look at the verse.

# LUKE 15:12

Great job! You got your next verse down!

You know the drill. Throughout your day when you're driving to work, taking a break from work, or cooking a meal, go over what you've memorized so far to keep reinforcing it in your mind.

Tomorrow you'll quickly review what you learned today and add another verse to it.

If you don't feel confident you've truly memorized today's verse, consider listening through the chapter again.

See you tomorrow!

Good Bless

# Luke 15:13

Today we are going to memorize Luke 15:13.

After you review what you have already learned, you are going to memorize today's verse using the 10-10-10 Method.

Let's begin.

Let's review the verse you learned yesterday by reciting it 10 times from memory. Glance over it if you need a refresher.

**"'And the younger of them said to his father, "Father, give me the share of property that is coming to me." And he divided his property between them'" (Luke 15:12).**

Now you're going to review all the verses you have memorized up to this point by reciting them 10 times. You can find it in the prep work chapter for this week if you need a refresher. If after three times you feel confident in your ability to recite all the verses you have currently memorized, feel free to call it good enough.

When your review is done, let's get into today's verse.

Say the following verse out loud 10 times:

"'Not many days later, the younger son gathered all he had and took a journey into a far country, and there he squandered his property in reckless living'" (Luke 15:13).

When you are done, recite the verse 10 times in a row from memory, doing your best not to look at the verse.

Great job! You got your next verse down!

You know the drill, throughout your day when you're driving to work, taking a break from work, or cooking a meal, go over what you've memorized so far to keep reinforcing it in your mind.

Tomorrow you'll quickly review what you learned today and add another verse to it.

If you don't feel confident you've truly memorized today's verse, consider listening through the chapter again.

See you tomorrow!

God bless.

# Luke 15:14

Today we are going to memorize Luke 15:14.

After you review what you have already learned, you are going to memorize today's verse using the 10-10-10 Method.

Let's begin.

Let's review the verse you learned yesterday by reciting it 10 times from memory. Glance over it if you need a refresher.

**"'Not many days later, the younger son gathered all he had and took a journey into a far country, and there he squandered his property in reckless living'" (Luke 15:13).**

Now you're going to review all the verses you have memorized up to this point by reciting them 10 times. You can find it in the prep work chapter for this week if you need a refresher. If after three times you feel confident in your ability to recite all the verses you have currently memorized, feel free to call it good enough.

When your review is done, let's get into today's verse.

Say the following verse out loud 10 times:

**"'And when he had spent everything, a severe famine arose in that country, and he began to be in need'" (Luke 15:14).**

When you are done, recite the verse 10 times in a row from memory, doing your best not to look at the verse.

Great job! You got your next verse down!

You know the drill, throughout your day when you're driving to work, taking a break from work, or cooking a meal, go over what you've memorized so far to keep reinforcing it in your mind.

Tomorrow you'll quickly review what you learned today and add another verse to it.

If you don't feel confident you've truly memorized today's verse, consider listening through the chapter again.

See you tomorrow!
  God bless.

# Luke 15:15

Today we are going to memorize Luke 15:15.

After you review what you have already learned, you are going to memorize today's verse using the 10-10-10 Method.

Let's begin.

Let's review the verse you learned yesterday by reciting it 10 times from memory. Glance over it if you need a refresher.

**"'And when he had spent everything, a severe famine arose in that country, and he began to be in need'" (Luke 15:14).**

Now you're going to review all the verses you have memorized up to this point by reciting them 10 times. You can find it in the prep work chapter for this week if you need a refresher. If after three times you feel confident in your ability to recite all the verses you have currently memorized, feel free to call it good enough.

When your review is done, let's get into today's verse.

Say the following verse out loud 10 times:

**"'So he went and hired himself out to one of the citizens of that country, who sent him into his fields to feed pigs'" (Luke 15:15).**

When you are done, recite the verse 10 times in a row from memory, doing your best not to look at the verse.

Great job! You got your next verse down!

You know the drill, throughout your day when you're driving to work, taking a break from work, or cooking a meal, go over what you've memorized so far to keep reinforcing it in your mind.

Tomorrow you'll quickly review what you learned today and add another verse to it.

If you don't feel confident you've truly memorized today's verse, consider listening through the chapter again.

See you tomorrow!

God bless.

# Luke 15:16

Today we are going to memorize Luke 15:16.

After you review what you have already learned, you are going to memorize today's verse using the 10-10-10 Method.

Let's begin.

Let's review the verse you learned yesterday by reciting it 10 times from memory. Glance over it if you need a refresher.

**"'So he went and hired himself out to one of the citizens of that country, who sent him into his fields to feed pigs'" (Luke 15:15).**

Now you're going to review all the verses you have memorized up to this point by reciting them 10 times. You can find it in the prep work chapter for this week if you need a refresher. If after three times you feel confident in your ability to recite all the verses you have currently memorized, feel free to call it good enough.

When your review is done, let's get into today's verse.

Say the following verse out loud 10 times:

**"'And he was longing to be fed with the pods that the pigs ate, and no one gave him anything'" (Luke 15:16).**

When you are done, recite the verse 10 times in a row from memory, doing your best not to look at the verse.

Great job! You got your next verse down and your first block of 6 verses, too!

With your first block of verses completed, I would love to hear what you think so far about the book in the form of a review.

Reviews help other listeners find this book so that they too can become more intimate with God's Word.

Better yet, leaving a review is easy.

Simply go to the book's page on Amazon, scroll down and click the 'leave a customer review' button, choose a rating, leave a few words, and you're done!

Bonus points for leaving a picture with your review.

Super bonus points for a video.

Just a few minutes of your time will help people from all over the world, people you may never meet in this life, find this book and seal God's Word in their hearts.

Tomorrow you have the optional prep work for the next block of 6 verses. Though it's not mandatory, I can't stress enough how beneficial it will be moving forward.

If you plan to skip it, simply move to the following chapter to begin memorizing the first verse of the next block of 6 verses.

See you tomorrow!

God Bless!

# Week 2 Prep Work

If you are here, that tells me you are ready for your next block of verses to memorize.

Great job so far. I know it takes a lot of time and effort to memorize scripture and I hope all that time and effort has been a joyful experience.

Just like with the first round of prep work, this is completely optional.

You are not required to do this to memorize the next block of 6 verses.

But like I said before, it will make the task much easier.

If you are not up for the prep work, feel free to skip this chapter.

If you are willing to give it a shot, get ready to read the next 6 verses out loud 50 times which will take you about an hour.

If you don't have an hour, run through them 25 times which will only take you about 30 minutes.

Or commit to whatever you can.

Anything and everything you do here will help moving forward.

## MEMORIZING THE PARABLE OF THE PRODIGAL SON

Please note, I left the verse numbers in the passage for your reference only.

When you are ready, begin.

17 "But when he came to himself, he said, 'How many of my father's hired servants have more than enough bread, but I perish here with hunger! 18 I will arise and go to my father, and I will say to him, "Father, I have sinned against heaven and before you. 19 I am no longer worthy to be called your son. Treat me as one of your hired servants."' 20 And he arose and came to his father. But while he was still a long way off, his father saw him and felt compassion, and ran and embraced him and kissed him. 21 And the son said to him, 'Father, I have sinned against heaven and before you. I am no longer worthy to be called your son.' 22 But the father said to his servants, 'Bring quickly the best robe, and put it on him, and put a ring on his hand, and shoes on his feet.'" (Luke 15:17-22)

See you tomorrow!

# Luke 15:17

Today we are going to memorize Luke 15:17.

After you review what you have already learned, you are going to memorize today's verse using the 10-10-10 Method.

Let's begin.

Let's review the verse you learned last by reciting it 10 times from memory. Glance over it if you need a refresher.

**"'And he was longing to be fed with the pods that the pigs ate, and no one gave him anything'" (Luke 15:16).**

Now you're going to review all the verses you have memorized up to this point by reciting them 10 times. You can find it in the prep work chapter for this week if you need a refresher. If after three times you feel confident in your ability to recite all the verses you have currently memorized, feel free to call it good enough.

When your review is done, let's get into today's verse.

Say the following verse out loud 10 times:

**"'But when he came to himself, he said, "How many of my father's hired servants have more than enough bread, but I perish here with hunger!"'"
(Luke 15:17).**

When you are done, recite the verse 10 times in a row from memory, doing your best not to look at the verse.

Great job! You got your next verse down!

You know the drill, throughout your day when you're driving to work, taking a break from work, or cooking a meal, go over what you've memorized so far to keep reinforcing it in your mind.

Tomorrow you'll quickly review what you learned today and add another verse to it.

If you don't feel confident you've truly memorized today's verse, consider listening through the chapter again.

See you tomorrow!

God bless.

# Luke 15:18

Today we are going to memorize Luke 15:18.

After you review what you have already learned, you are going to memorize today's verse using the 10-10-10 Method.

Let's begin.

Let's review the verse you learned yesterday by reciting it 10 times from memory. Glance over it if you need a refresher.

**"'But when he came to himself, he said, "How many of my father's hired servants have more than enough bread, but I perish here with hunger!"'" (Luke 15:17).**

Now you're going to review all the verses you have memorized up to this point by reciting them 10 times. You can find it in the prep work chapter for this week if you need a refresher. If after three times you feel confident in your ability to recite all the verses you have currently memorized, feel free to call it good enough.

When your review is done, let's get into today's verse.

Say the following verse out loud 10 times:

**""'I will arise and go to my father, and I will say to him, 'Father, I have sinned against heaven and before you'"'" (Luke 15:18).**

When you are done, recite the verse 10 times in a row from memory, doing your best not to look at the verse.

Great job! You got your next verse down!

You know the drill, throughout your day when you're driving to work, taking a break from work, or cooking a meal, go over what you've memorized so far to keep reinforcing it in your mind.

Tomorrow you'll quickly review what you learned today and add another verse to it.

If you don't feel confident you've truly memorized today's verse, consider listening through the chapter again.

See you tomorrow!

God bless.

# Luke 15:19

Today we are going to memorize Luke 15:19.

After you review what you have already learned, you are going to memorize today's verse using the 10-10-10 Method.

Let's begin.

Let's review the verse you learned yesterday by reciting it 10 times from memory. Glance over it if you need a refresher.

**""'I will arise and go to my father, and I will say to him, 'Father, I have sinned against heaven and before you'""" (Luke 15:18).**

Now you're going to review all the verses you have memorized up to this point by reciting them 10 times. You can find it in the prep work chapter for this week if you need a refresher. If after three times you feel confident in your ability to recite all the verses you have currently memorized, feel free to call it good enough.

When your review is done, let's get into today's verse.

Say the following verse out loud 10 times:

"""'I am no longer worthy to be called your son. Treat me as one of your hired servants'"""** (Luke 15:19).

When you are done, recite the verse 10 times in a row from memory, doing your best not to look at the verse.

Great job! You got your next verse down!

You know the drill, throughout your day when you're driving to work, taking a break from work, or cooking a meal, go over what you've memorized so far to keep reinforcing it in your mind.

Tomorrow you'll quickly review what you learned today and add another verse to it.

If you don't feel confident you've truly memorized today's verse, consider listening through the chapter again.

See you tomorrow!

God bless.

# Luke 15:20

Today we are going to memorize Luke 15:20.

After you review what you have already learned, you are going to memorize today's verse using the 10-10-10 Method.

Let's begin.

Let's review the verse you learned yesterday by reciting it 10 times from memory. Glance over it if you need a refresher.

**"""'I am no longer worthy to be called your son. Treat me as one of your hired servants'"""** (Luke 15:19).

Now you're going to review all the verses you have memorized up to this point by reciting them 10 times. You can find it in the prep work chapter for this week if you need a refresher. If after three times you feel confident in your ability to recite all the verses you have currently memorized, feel free to call it good enough.

When your review is done, let's get into today's verse.

Say the following verse out loud 10 times:

**"'And he arose and came to his father. But while he was still a long way off, his father saw him and felt compassion, and ran and embraced him and kissed him'" (Luke 15:20).**

When you are done, recite the verse 10 times in a row from memory, doing your best not to look at the verse.

Great job! You got your next verse down!

You know the drill, throughout your day when you're driving to work, taking a break from work, or cooking a meal, go over what you've memorized so far to keep reinforcing it in your mind.

Tomorrow you'll quickly review what you learned today and add another verse to it.

If you don't feel confident you've truly memorized today's verse, consider listening through the chapter again.

See you tomorrow!

God bless.

# Luke 15:21

Today we are going to memorize Luke 15:21.

After you review what you have already learned, you are going to memorize today's verse using the 10-10-10 Method.

Let's begin.

Let's review the verse you learned yesterday by reciting it 10 times from memory. Glance over it if you need a refresher.

**"'And he arose and came to his father. But while he was still a long way off, his father saw him and felt compassion, and ran and embraced him and kissed him'" (Luke 15:20).**

Now you're going to review all the verses you have memorized up to this point by reciting them 10 times. You can find it in the prep work chapter for this week if you need a refresher. If after three times you feel confident in your ability to recite all the verses you have currently memorized, feel free to call it good enough.

When your review is done, let's get into today's verse.

Say the following verse out loud 10 times:

**"'And the son said to him, "Father, I have sinned against heaven and before you. I am no longer worthy to be called your son"'"** (Luke 15:21).

When you are done, recite the verse 10 times in a row from memory, doing your best not to look at the verse.

Great job! You got your next verse down!

You know the drill, throughout your day when you're driving to work, taking a break from work, or cooking a meal, go over what you've memorized so far to keep reinforcing it in your mind.

Tomorrow you'll quickly review what you learned today and add another verse to it.

If you don't feel confident you've truly memorized today's verse, consider listening through the chapter again.

See you tomorrow!

God bless.

# Luke 15:22

Today we are going to memorize Luke 15:22.

After you review what you have already learned, you are going to memorize today's verse using the 10-10-10 Method.

Let's begin.

Let's review the verse you learned yesterday by reciting it 10 times from memory. Glance over it if you need a refresher.

**"'And the son said to him, "Father, I have sinned against heaven and before you. I am no longer worthy to be called your son"'" (Luke 15:21).**

Now you're going to review all the verses you have memorized up to this point by reciting them 10 times. You can find it in the prep work chapter for this week if you need a refresher. If after three times you feel confident in your ability to recite all the verses you have currently memorized, feel free to call it good enough.

When your review is done, let's get into today's verse.

Say the following verse out loud 10 times:

**"'But the father said to his servants, "Bring quickly the best robe, and put it on him, and put a ring on his hand, and shoes on his feet"'" (Luke 15:22).**

When you are done, recite the verse 10 times in a row from memory, doing your best not to look at the verse.

Great job! You got your next verse down!

You know the drill, throughout your day when you're driving to work, taking a break from work, or cooking a meal, go over what you've memorized so far to keep reinforcing it in your mind.

Tomorrow you have the optional prep work for the next block of 6 verses. Though it's not mandatory, I can't stress enough how beneficial it will be moving forward.

If you plan to skip it, simply move to the following chapter to begin memorizing the first verse of the next block of 6 verses.

If you don't feel confident you've truly memorized today's verse, consider listening through the chapter again.

See you tomorrow!

God bless.

# Week 3 Prep Work

If you are here, that tells me you are ready for your next block of verses to memorize.

Great job so far. I know it takes a lot of time and effort to memorize scripture and I hope all that time and effort has been a joyful experience.

Just like with the first round of prep work, this is completely optional.

You are not required to do this to memorize the next block of 6 verses.

But like I said before, it will make the task much easier.

If you are not up for the prep work, feel free to skip this chapter.

If you are willing to give it a shot, get ready to read the next 6 verses out loud 50 times which will take you about an hour.

If you don't have an hour, run through them 25 times which will only take you about 30 minutes.

Or commit to whatever you can.

Anything and everything you do here will help moving forward.

Please note, I left the verse numbers in the passage for your reference only.

When you are ready, begin.

23 "'And bring the fattened calf and kill it, and let us eat and celebrate. 24 For this my son was dead, and is alive again; he was lost, and is found.' And they began to celebrate. 25 Now his older son was in the field, and as he came and drew near to the house, he heard music and dancing. 26 And he called one of the servants and asked what these things meant. 27 And he said to him, 'Your brother has come, and your father has killed the fattened calf, because he has received him back safe and sound.' 28 But he was angry and refused to go in. His father came out and entreated him." (Luke 15:23-28)

See you tomorrow!

# Luke 15:23

Today we are going to memorize Luke 15:23.

After you review what you have already learned, you are going to memorize today's verse using the 10-10-10 Method.

Let's begin.

Let's review the verse you learned yesterday by reciting it 10 times from memory. Glance over it if you need a refresher.

**"'But the father said to his servants, "Bring quickly the best robe, and put it on him, and put a ring on his hand, and shoes on his feet"'" (Luke 15:22).**

Now you're going to review all the verses you have memorized up to this point by reciting them 10 times. You can find it in the prep work chapter for this week if you need a refresher. If after three times you feel confident in your ability to recite all the verses you have currently memorized, feel free to call it good enough.

When your review is done, let's get into today's verse.

Say the following verse out loud 10 times:

"'"And bring the fattened calf and kill it, and let us eat and celebrate"'" (Luke 15:23).

When you are done, recite the verse 10 times in a row from memory, doing your best not to look at the verse.

Great job! You got your next verse down!

You know the drill, throughout your day when you're driving to work, taking a break from work, or cooking a meal, go over what you've memorized so far to keep reinforcing it in your mind.

Tomorrow you'll quickly review what you learned today and add another verse to it.

If you don't feel confident you've truly memorized today's verse, consider listening through the chapter again.

See you tomorrow!

God bless.

# Luke 15:24

Today we are going to memorize Luke 15:24.

After you review what you have already learned, you are going to memorize today's verse using the 10-10-10 Method.

Let's begin.

Let's review the verse you learned last by reciting it 10 times from memory. Glance over it if you need a refresher.

**"'"And bring the fattened calf and kill it, and let us eat and celebrate"'"** **(Luke 15:23).**

Now you're going to review all the verses you have memorized up to this point by reciting them 10 times. You can find it in the prep work chapter for this week if you need a refresher. If after three times you feel confident in your ability to recite all the verses you have currently memorized, feel free to call it good enough.

When your review is done, let's get into today's verse.

Say the following verse out loud 10 times:

**"'"For this my son was dead, and is alive again; he was lost, and is found." And they began to celebrate'" (Luke 15:24).**

When you are done, recite the verse 10 times in a row from memory, doing your best not to look at the verse.

Great job! You got your next verse down!

You know the drill, throughout your day when you're driving to work, taking a break from work, or cooking a meal, go over what you've memorized so far to keep reinforcing it in your mind.

Tomorrow you'll quickly review what you learned today and add another verse to it.

If you don't feel confident you've truly memorized today's verse, consider listening through the chapter again.

See you tomorrow!

God bless.

# Luke 15:25

Today we are going to memorize Luke 15:25.

After you review what you have already learned, you are going to memorize today's verse using the 10-10-10 Method.

Let's begin.

Let's review the verse you learned yesterday by reciting it 10 times from memory. Glance over it if you need a refresher.

"'"For this my son was dead, and is alive again; he was lost, and is found." And they began to celebrate'" (Luke 15:24).

Now you're going to review all the verses you have memorized up to this point by reciting them 10 times. You can find it in the prep work chapter for this week if you need a refresher. If after three times you feel confident in your ability to recite all the verses you have currently memorized, feel free to call it good enough.

When your review is done, let's get into today's verse.

Say the following verse out loud 10 times:

**"'Now his older son was in the field, and as he came and drew near to the house, he heard music and dancing'" (Luke 15:25).**

When you are done, recite the verse 10 times in a row from memory, doing your best not to look at the verse.

Great job! You got your next verse down!

You know the drill, throughout your day when you're driving to work, taking a break from work, or cooking a meal, go over what you've memorized so far to keep reinforcing it in your mind.

Tomorrow you'll quickly review what you learned today and add another verse to it.

If you don't feel confident you've truly memorized today's verse, consider listening through the chapter again.

See you tomorrow!

God bless.

# Luke 15:26

Today we are going to memorize Luke 15:26.

After you review what you have already learned, you are going to memorize today's verse using the 10-10-10 Method.

Let's begin.

Let's review the verse you learned yesterday by reciting it 10 times from memory. Glance over it if you need a refresher.

**"'Now his older son was in the field, and as he came and drew near to the house, he heard music and dancing'" (Luke 15:25).**

Now you're going to review all the verses you have memorized up to this point by reciting them 10 times. You can find it in the prep work chapter for this week if you need a refresher. If after three times you feel confident in your ability to recite all the verses you have currently memorized, feel free to call it good enough.

When your review is done, let's get into today's verse.

Say the following verse out loud 10 times:

**"'And he called one of the servants and asked what these things meant'" (Luke 15:26).**

When you are done, recite the verse 10 times in a row from memory, doing your best not to look at the verse.

Great job! You got your next verse down!

You know the drill, throughout your day when you're driving to work, taking a break from work, or cooking a meal, go over what you've memorized so far to keep reinforcing it in your mind.

Tomorrow you'll quickly review what you learned today and add another verse to it.

If you don't feel confident you've truly memorized today's verse, consider listening through the chapter again.

See you tomorrow!

God bless.

# Luke 15:27

Today we are going to memorize Luke 15:27.

After you review what you have already learned, you are going to memorize today's verse using the 10-10-10 Method.

Let's begin.

Let's review the verse you learned yesterday by reciting it 10 times from memory. Glance over it if you need a refresher.

**"'And he called one of the servants and asked what these things meant'" (Luke 15:26).**

Now you're going to review all the verses you have memorized up to this point by reciting them 10 times. You can find it in the prep work chapter for this week if you need a refresher. If after three times you feel confident in your ability to recite all the verses you have currently memorized, feel free to call it good enough.

When your review is done, let's get into today's verse.

Say the following verse out loud 10 times:

**"'And he said to him, "Your brother has come, and your father has killed the fattened calf, because he has received him back safe and sound"'"** (Luke 15:27).

When you are done, recite the verse 10 times in a row from memory, doing your best not to look at the verse.

Great job! You got your next verse down!

You know the drill, throughout your day when you're driving to work, taking a break from work, or cooking a meal, go over what you've memorized so far to keep reinforcing it in your mind.

Tomorrow you'll quickly review what you learned today and add another verse to it.

If you don't feel confident you've truly memorized today's verse, consider listening through the chapter again.

See you tomorrow!

God bless.

# Luke 15:28

Today we are going to memorize Luke 15:28.

After you review what you have already learned, you are going to memorize today's verse using the 10-10-10 Method.

Let's begin.

Let's review the verse you learned yesterday by reciting it 10 times from memory. Glance over it if you need a refresher.

**"'And he said to him, "Your brother has come, and your father has killed the fattened calf, because he has received him back safe and sound"'" (Luke 15:27).**

Now you're going to review all the verses you have memorized up to this point by reciting them 10 times. You can find it in the prep work chapter for this week if you need a refresher. If after three times you feel confident in your ability to recite all the verses you have currently memorized, feel free to call it good enough.

When your review is done, let's get into today's verse.

Say the following verse out loud 10 times:

**"'But he was angry and refused to go in. His father came out and entreated him'" (Luke 15:28).**

When you are done, recite the verse 10 times in a row from memory, doing your best not to look at the verse.

Great job! You got your next verse down!

You know the drill, throughout your day when you're driving to work, taking a break from work, or cooking a meal, go over what you've memorized so far to keep reinforcing it in your mind.

Tomorrow you have the optional prep work for the last block of 4 verses. Though it's not mandatory, I can't stress enough how beneficial it will be moving forward.

If you plan to skip it, simply move to the following chapter to begin memorizing the first verse of the last block of 4 verses.

If you don't feel confident you've truly memorized today's verse, consider listening through the chapter again.

See you tomorrow!

God bless.

# Week 4 Prep Work

If you are here, that tells me you are ready for your last block of verses to memorize.

Great job so far. I know it takes a lot of time and effort to memorize scripture and I hope all that time and effort has been a joyful experience.

Just like with the first round of prep work, this is completely optional.

You are not required to do this to memorize the last block of 4 verses.

But like I said before, it will make the task much easier.

If you are not up for the prep work, feel free to skip this chapter.

If you are willing to give it a shot, get ready to read the last 4 verses out loud 50 times which will take you about 40 minutes.

If you don't have 40 minutes to spare, run through them 25 times which will only take you about 20 minutes.

Or commit to whatever you can.

Anything and everything you do here will help moving forward.

Please note, I left the verse numbers in the passage for your reference only.

When you are ready, begin.

29 "But he answered his father, 'Look, these many years I have served you, and I never disobeyed your command, yet you never gave me a young goat, that I might celebrate with my friends. 30 But when this son of yours came, who has devoured your property with prostitutes, you killed the fattened calf for him!' 31 And he said to him, 'Son, you are always with me, and all that is mine is yours. 32 It was fitting to celebrate and be glad, for this your brother was dead, and is alive; he was lost, and is found.'" (Luke 15:29-32)

See you tomorrow!

# Luke 15:29

Today we are going to memorize Luke 15:29.

After you review what you have already learned, you are going to memorize today's verse using the 10-10-10 Method.

Let's begin.

Let's review the verse you learned yesterday by reciting it 10 times from memory. Glance over it if you need a refresher.

**"'But he was angry and refused to go in. His father came out and entreated him'" (Luke 15:28).**

Now you're going to review all the verses you have memorized up to this point by reciting them 10 times. You can find it in the prep work chapter for this week if you need a refresher. If after three times you feel confident in your ability to recite all the verses you have currently memorized, feel free to call it good enough.

When your review is done, let's get into today's verse.

Say the following verse out loud 10 times:

"'But he answered his father, "Look, these many years I have served you, and I never disobeyed your command, yet you never gave me a young goat, that I might celebrate with my friends"'" (Luke 15:29).

When you are done, recite the verse 10 times in a row from memory, doing your best not to look at the verse.

Great job! You got your next verse down!

You know the drill, throughout your day when you're driving to work, taking a break from work, or cooking a meal, go over what you've memorized so far to keep reinforcing it in your mind.

Tomorrow you'll quickly review what you learned today and add another verse to it.

If you don't feel confident you've truly memorized today's verse, consider listening through the chapter again.

See you tomorrow!

God bless.

# Luke 15:30

Today we are going to memorize Luke 15:30.

After you review what you have already learned, you are going to memorize today's verse using the 10-10-10 Method.

Let's begin.

Let's review the verse you learned yesterday by reciting it 10 times from memory. Glance over it if you need a refresher.

**"'But he answered his father, "Look, these many years I have served you, and I never disobeyed your command, yet you never gave me a young goat, that I might celebrate with my friends"'" (Luke 15:29).**

Now you're going to review all the verses you have memorized up to this point by reciting them 10 times. You can find it in the prep work chapter for this week if you need a refresher. If after three times you feel confident in your ability to recite all the verses you have currently memorized, feel free to call it good enough.

When your review is done, let's get into today's verse.

Say the following verse out loud 10 times:

**"'"But when this son of yours came, who has devoured your property with prostitutes, you killed the fattened calf for him!"'"** (Luke 15:30).

When you are done, recite the verse 10 times in a row from memory, doing your best not to look at the verse.

Great job! You got your next verse down!

You know the drill, throughout your day when you're driving to work, taking a break from work, or cooking a meal, go over what you've memorized so far to keep reinforcing it in your mind.

Tomorrow you'll quickly review what you learned today and add another verse to it.

If you don't feel confident you've truly memorized today's verse, consider listening through the chapter again.

See you tomorrow!

God bless!

# Luke 15:31

Today we are going to memorize Luke 15:31.

After you review what you have already learned, you are going to memorize today's verse using the 10-10-10 Method.

Let's begin.

Let's review the verse you learned yesterday by reciting it 10 times from memory. Glance over it if you need a refresher.

""'But when this son of yours came, who has devoured your property with prostitutes, you killed the fattened calf for him!'"" (Luke 15:30).

Now you're going to review all the verses you have memorized up to this point by reciting them 10 times. You can find it in the prep work chapter for this week if you need a refresher. If after three times you feel confident in your ability to recite all the verses you have currently memorized, feel free to call it good enough.

When your review is done, let's get into today's verse.

Say the following verse out loud 10 times:

**"'And he said to him, "Son, you are always with me, and all that is mine is yours"'" (Luke 15:31).**

When you are done, recite the verse 10 times in a row from memory, doing your best not to look at the verse.

Great job! You got your next verse down!

You know the drill, throughout your day when you're driving to work, taking a break from work, or cooking a meal, go over what you've memorized so far to keep reinforcing it in your mind.

Tomorrow you'll quickly review what you learned today and add another verse to it.

If you don't feel confident you've truly memorized today's verse, consider listening through the chapter again.

See you tomorrow!

God bless.

# Luke 15:32

Today we are going to memorize Luke 15:32.

After you review what you have already learned, you are going to memorize today's verse using the 10-10-10 Method.

Let's begin.

Let's review the verse you learned yesterday by reciting it 10 times from memory. Glance over it if you need a refresher.

**"'And he said to him, "Son, you are always with me, and all that is mine is yours"'" (Luke 15:31).**

Now you're going to review all the verses you have memorized up to this point by reciting them 10 times. You can find it in the prep work chapter for this week if you need a refresher. If after three times you feel confident in your ability to recite all the verses you have currently memorized, feel free to call it good enough.

When your review is done, let's get into today's verse.

Say the following verse out loud 10 times:

**"'"It was fitting to celebrate and be glad, for this your brother was dead, and is alive; he was lost, and is found"'" (Luke 15:32).**

When you are done, recite the verse 10 times in a row from memory, doing your best not to look at the verse.

Great job! You got your last verse down!

You know the drill, throughout your day when you are driving your car, taking a break from work, or cooking a meal, go over what you have memorized so far to keep reinforcing it in your mind.

If by chance you don't feel confident you have truly memorized today's verse, consider listening through the chapter again.

God Bless!

# Conclusion

If you are here, I hope that means you have fully memorized the parable of the Prodigal Son.

I hope the experience was rewarding and enriching as you sealed part of God's Word in your heart.

I recommend reciting the full passage every day for the next 30 days to truly solidify that piece of scripture in your mind.

Once you're done, consider memorizing another passage or even an entire book of the Bible!

Lastly, if you have enjoyed this book, do consider leaving a review. I look forward to seeing your feedback.

May God bless you on your journey to further know Him, and I leave you with these two verses, "All Scripture is breathed out by God and profitable for teaching, for reproof, for correction, and for training in righteousness, that the man of God may be complete, equipped for every good work" (2 Timothy 3:16-17).

www.ingramcontent.com/pod-product-compliance
Lightning Source LLC
Chambersburg PA
CBHW030138100526
44592CB00011B/947